Pentimento of Narcissus

(Poem and Commentary)

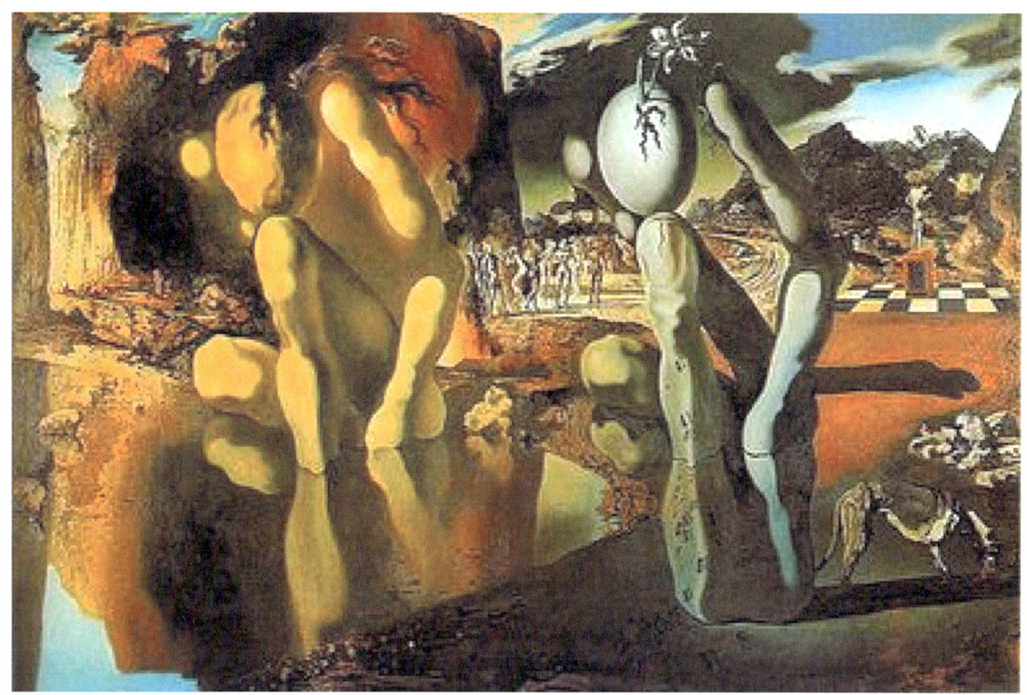

Salvador Dalí, *Metamorphosis of Narcissus*, 1938

Henning K. Schmsdorf

Printed by Applied Digital Imaging, Bellingham, WA

Prolog

Psychotherapists and cultural pundits tell us today that contemporary society is fundamentally narcissistic. The therapeutic concept of Narcissism was propagated by Sigmund Freud in 1914, building on his immediate predecessors who had linked narcissistic personality traits with criminal homosexuality. In Freud's thinking, the story of Narcissus became the paradigm by which to distinguish infantile stirrings of libidinous energies set against the parental authority charged with instilling the social code in the child, and saddling "Its Majesty, the Baby" with a sense of guilt. Once the child learned to project its need for love on somebody beyond itself, the sense of guilt would abate in the mature adult. If, however, that maturation process for some reason was disturbed, the adult would suffer from pathological narcissism curable by therapy.

Freud's use of the Narcissus allegory as found in Ovid's *Metamorphoses* ignored two significant aspects of the ancient myth, first its linkage to the orbit of the goat-god, half nature and half man, and second that Narcissus' death from staring into the pool of his own self would produce the chaste flower of artistic creation. By contrast, C.G. Jung would argue that the myth of Narcissus in its fullest sense depicts the liminal experience of delving into the pre-conscious self, which is the perpetual and universal source of dreams, art, religion, and philosophy.

These meanings were adumbrated by the Symbolist artists and writers of second half of the nineteenth century, but were ignored in Freud's thinking. His analysis focused on the personal unconscious of the isolated individual. With the cultural shifts taking place in Western society since the 1970s, the individual, stripped of permanent cultural models identified with parental authority, finds itself confronted with substitute imagoes proffered by commercial media. Instead of feeling "guilt" from an internal judgement vis-a-vis the parent, the modern child and adolescent feel "shame" from not measuring up to the cultural images imposed online.

The poem below sets out to restore the ancient context of the Narcissus myth, followed by commentaries drawn from the primary sources on which the Narcissus tradition is based, and on modern discussions of the figure as it appears in contemporary psychodynamic therapy and social theory.

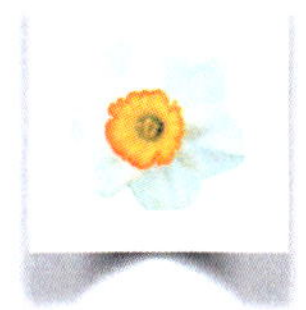

Narcissus
(with regrets to Freudian revisionists)

Narcissus —
Legendary brother,
How you've been shrunk!
Pitiful youth,
Drowning in your mirror image
In the pool of life.

How they forget!
The Arcadian satyr drinking from his own belly
Ingesting the midnight sun,
His demonic laughter
Shaking the Tree of Life,
Panicking shepherd and hunter to flight,
Beyond Good and Evil.

Pan alone in the reeds, playing his fluted lament,
Yearning for the Echo of his passion for the world,
Creating music from longing
for virginal Syrinx, Pitys, and Selene,
Moon Goddess in the sky.

Majestic Goat-God,
Son of Eros, Zeus, Hermes, or Apollo,
Child of chaste Penelope's rape,
Husband of Rhea, Mother of Earth,
World Spirit,
Orphic All, and Cosmic Eyeball!
Intoxicated priest of Dionysos!
Archetypal Man!

Melancholy warrior yearning for release,
Longing for transcendence.
Searching for Psyche within,
And turning into the chaste flower
Of the poet's inner vision —
Narcissus.

Commentary & Primary Sources (in approximately chronological order):

1. Arcadian Pan: Embodiment of nature's divinity in prehistoric, pre-agricultural Greece, specifically charged with animal fertility and sexual desire.

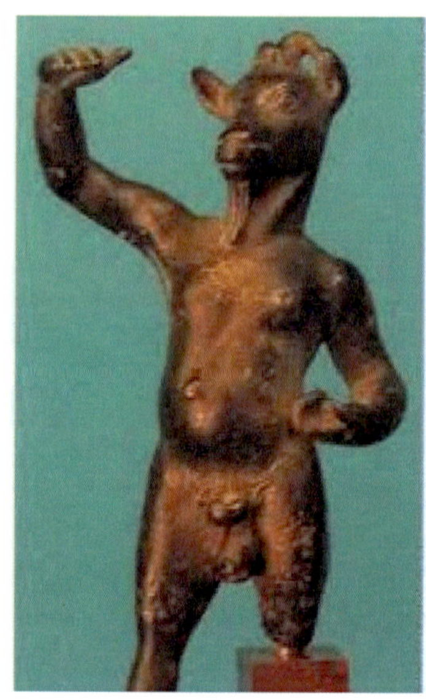

Pan, Goat-God of Arcadia
Lousoi Bronze (ca. 500 B.C.)

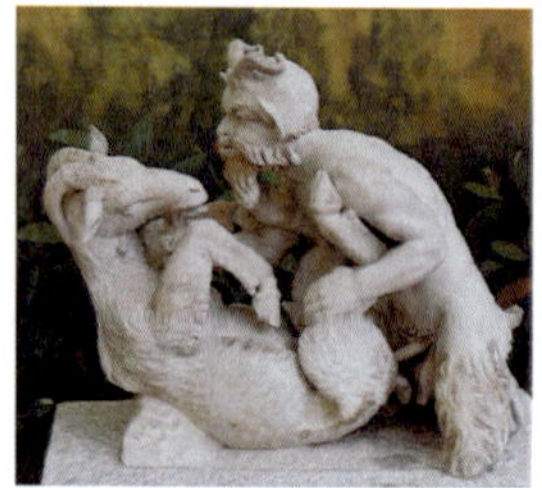

Pan impregnating goat,
1st century A.D.
Herculaneum, Italy

According to Herodotus (484 – 425 B.C.), Pan was the most ancient of the gods, preceding the Olympians. Alternately, Herodotus says that Pan was born just after the Trojan War, the son of the god Hermes and Penelope, a wood nymph. In evolutionary history, the genus Pan is part of the subfamily Homininae, which split into chimpanzees and humans ca. 5-12 million years ago.

2. Pan, lover of nymphs (Syrinx, Echo, Pitys) and the moon goddess, Selene. In various Greek and Roman legends, the god is associated with the etiology of certain plants (reeds, trees), the phenomenon of echo, and the origin of music.

Apuleius, *The Golden Ass* (2nd cent. A.D.) 5:25 : "The rustic god Pan sat on the brow of the stream, holding the mountain deity Echo in his arms, and teaching her to repeat after him all kinds of songs."

Nonnus, Dionysiaca (5th cent. A.D.) 16: 28 : "Goatherd Pan cried out : 'I wish my father had taught me the trick of that matchmaking wine! I wish I could be lord of the mind-tripping grape, like Bacchus! Then I should have seen that cruel maiden Echo, asleep and well drunken! Then I should have achieved my love, which like a gadfly sends me gadding afar! Farewell to this pasturage! For while I water my sheep here by a neighboring spring, Dionysos draws intractable Nymphs to marriage by means of his tippler's river! He has invented a medicine for Eros Love--his plant : away with the goat's milk, away with the milk of my ewes! For that cannot bring sleep to desire, nor a maiden to marriage. I alone, Aphrodite, must suffer. Alas for love! Syrinx escaped from Pan's marriage and left him without a bride, and now the pipes made from the plant [she was turned into] cries to the newly-made marriage of Dionysos with melodies unasked; while Syrinx gives voice, and to crown all, Echo chimes in with her familiar note. O Dionysos, charmer of mortals, shepherd of the bridal intoxication! you alone happy, because when the Nymph denied, you found out wine, love's helper to deck out the marriage!' Such were the words of Pan, in sorrow for his thwarted desire."

Virgil, (1st cent. B.C.) *Georgics* 3: 390: "With gift of snowy wool, Pan, Arcadia's god, charmed and beguiled you, O Moon [Selene], calling you to the depths of the woods; nor did you scorn his call."

Longus, (2nd cent. A.D.) *Daphnis and Chloe* (first novel in the Western canon). Longus weaves the legend of Pan's pursuit of Syrinx and how she was turned into the Pan pipes into the story of a young shepherd couple's sexual initiation. Pan appears as the god of shepherds and attendant in Dionysos' temple.

3. Pan as pederast. Pederasty in Archaic and Classical Greece was a socially acknowledged sexual relationship between a mature male (*erastes*=one who is loving) and a younger male (*eromenos*=one who is desired), marking ritualized passage into adulthood, with the older male becoming the instructor of the younger in archery, music, hunting and sports. The love for an *eromenos* is a frequent topic on Ancient Greek vases and in poems. The most famous pederastic relationship in Greek myth was that of Zeus for the human hero Ganymede (Homer, *Iliad*, 8th cent. B.C., book XX). While the modern use of the word pederasty implies the abuse of minors, Athenian law recognized both consent and age in regulating the practice.

4. Warrior and Athenian God: Historian Pausanias (*Description of Greece*, 2nd cent. A.D.) describes how the presence of Pan decided the outcome of a historical battle: "During the night there fell on them a 'panic.' For causeless terrors are said to come from the god Pan."

According to Herodotus (*Histories*, 6:105), Pan helped the Athenians defeat the invading Persians at the battle of Marathon (490 B.C.) by striking them with "panic," after which the cult of Pan was introduced at the city of Athens, and he became a major deity. Pan's role at Marathon can be construed as the chthonic power of the land eclipsing that of the foreign invader.

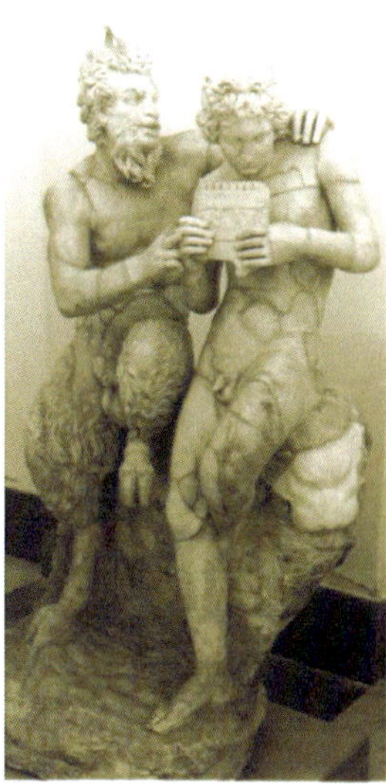
Pan teaching his *eromenos*, the shepherd Daphnis, to play the pan flute. Roman copy of Greek original c. 100 B.C., found in Pompeii.

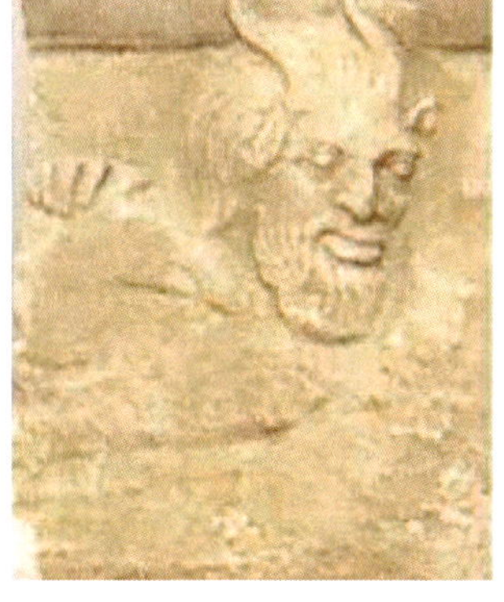
Head of Pan in votive panel, 5th century B.C.

5. Orphic Pan (Universal God): *Homeric Hymn to Pan* (7th or 6th B.C.) : "Muse, tell me about Pan, the dear son of Hermes, with his goat's feet and two horns…the shepherd god …he courses through the glistening high mountains, and often on the shouldering hills he speeds along slaying wild beasts, this keen-eyed god… As he returns from the chase, he sounds his note… while Echo cries… From his birth he was marvelous to look upon… all the immortals and Bacchanalian Dionysos were glad in heart and they called the boy Pan because he delighted all."

Anonymous Greek lyric (5 B.C.):
"I sing of Pan… All the earth and sea are one thanks to you, for you are the bulwark of all, oh, Pan, Pan!"

Orphic Hymn to Pan (3rd cent. B.C.):
 "I call strong Pan, the substance of the whole, etherial, marine, earthly, general soul,
Immortal fire; for all the world is thine, and all are parts of thee, O pow'r divine.
Come, blessed Pan, whom rural haunts delight, come, leaping, agile, wand'ring, starry light;
The Hours and Seasons, wait thy high command, and round thy throne in graceful order stand.
Goat-footed, horned, Bacchanalian Pan, fanatic pow'r, from whom the world began,
Whose various parts by thee inspir'd, combine in endless dance and melody divine.
In thee a refuge from our fears we find, those fears peculiar to the human

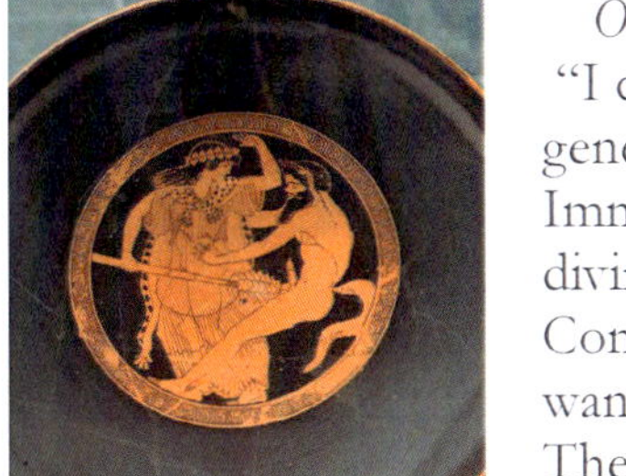
Female follower of Dionysos (*maenad*) and a satyr. Drinking cup, ca. 490–480 B.C.)

kind.
The shepherds, streams of water, goats rejoice, thou lov'st the chase, and Echo's secret voice:
The sportive nymphs, thy ev'ry step attend, and all thy works fulfill their destin'd end.
O all-producing pow'r, much-fam'd, divine, the world's great ruler, rich increase is thine.
All-fertile Pan, heav'nly splendor pure, in fruits rejoicing, and in caves obscure.
True serpent-horned Zeus, whose dreadful rage when rous'd, 'tis hard for mortals to assuage.
By thee the earth wide-bosom'd deep and long, stands on a basis permanent and strong.
Th' unwearied waters of the rolling sea, profoundly spreading, yield to thy decree.
Old Ocean [*Okeanos*] too reveres thy high command, whose liquid arms begirt the solid land.
The spacious air, whose nutrimental fire, and vivid blasts, the heat of life inspire
The lighter frame of fire, whose sparkling eye shines on the summit of the azure sky,
Submit alike to thee, whole general sway all parts of matter, various form'd obey.
All nature's change thro' thy protecting care, and all mankind thy lib'ral bounties share:
For these where'er dispers'd thro' boundless space, still find thy providence support their race.
Come, Bacchanalian, blessed power draw near, fanatic Pan, thy humble suppliant hear,
Propitious to these holy rites attend, and grant my life may meet a prosp'rous end;
Drive panic Fury too, wherever found, from human kind, to earth's remotest bound.

6. Dionysian Pan: The god of vegetation, fertility, fruit, wine, feasting, insanity, ritual
madness, religious ecstasy, and theatre, Dionysos (Διόνυσος) represented a release from the

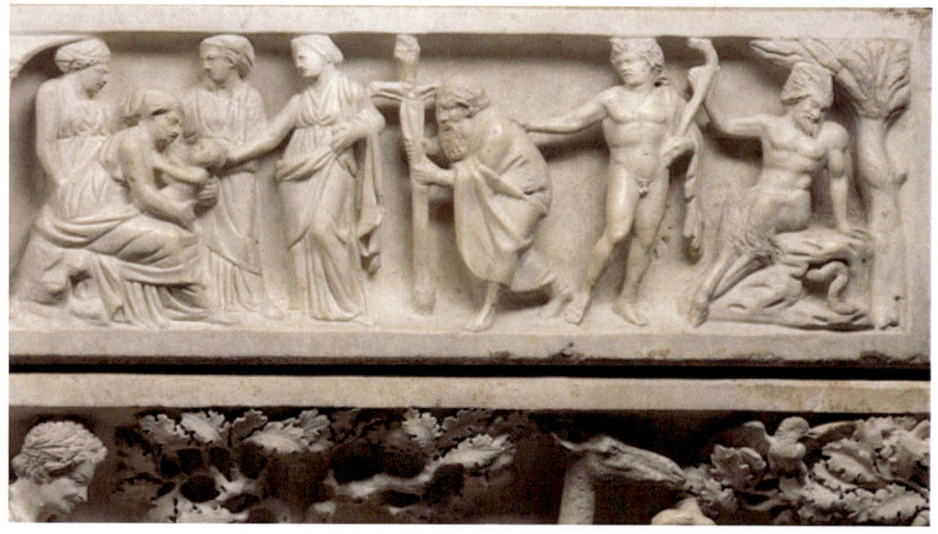

Marble sarcophagus with the Triumph of Dionysos (detail: Dionysos and Pan, on the left Cybele). Late Imperial
Rome, 260–270 A.D.

constraints of society's rules and encroachments of civilization, the diametric opposite to Apollo,
the god of measure and balance. One of the earliest gods attested in Mycenaean culture (circa
1750-1050 B.C.), the first two syllables of his name simply mean "god." The Romans called
him Bacchus for the frenzy he induced through rituals involving wine, music, and ecstatic dance
(*bacchanalia*).

In his role as warrior, Pan was drawn into the orbit of orgiastic Dionysos, and aided him on his
military expeditions to India, where Dionysos established settlements and taught the cultivation of

wine, and to Phrygia in pre-Hellenic Asia Minor (today Turkey), where Dionysos was inducted into the mystery rites of Cybele, the Great Mother goddess. Returned to Greece, Dionysos become the driving force behind the development of theatre rooted in the bacchanalian worship rituals in which the satyr (τραγῳδία=goat song) played a significant role (as first described by Friedrich Nietzsche — see below).

6. In Imperial Rome, goat-legged Pan was often conflated with Silvanus and Faunus (Virgil, 70-19 B.C, *Aeneid),* but eventually evolved into a naked youth and warrior longing for transcendence from animal nature.

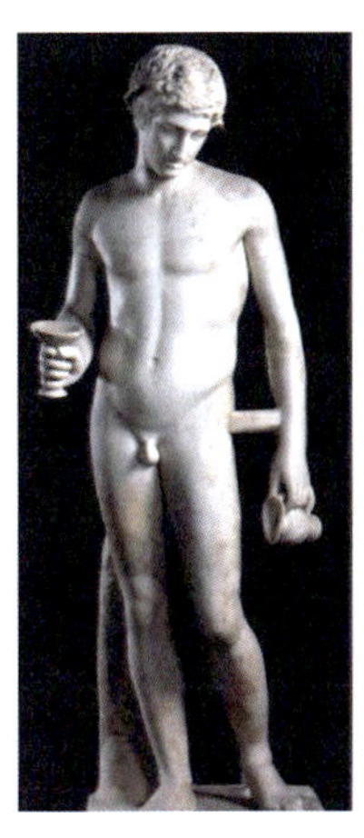

Pan as naked youth (small goat-horns sprouting from his head), a cup in each hand.
45-25 B.C., Imperial Rome

7. Pan and Narcissus. Narcissus and his twin sister Echo were the children of the river god Cephissus and the nymph Liriope, Like their sisters, the naiads or nymphs, they were part of a large group of nature spirits inhabiting all rivers and streams of the earth. The satyrs, pans and nymphs were descendants of Oceanus, the physical manifestation of the globe-encircling river (sea). As spirits or "demons" (δαίμονες) of the mountains and highland pastures, they protected the goatherds and sheep flocks which grazed these lands, and their human owners and

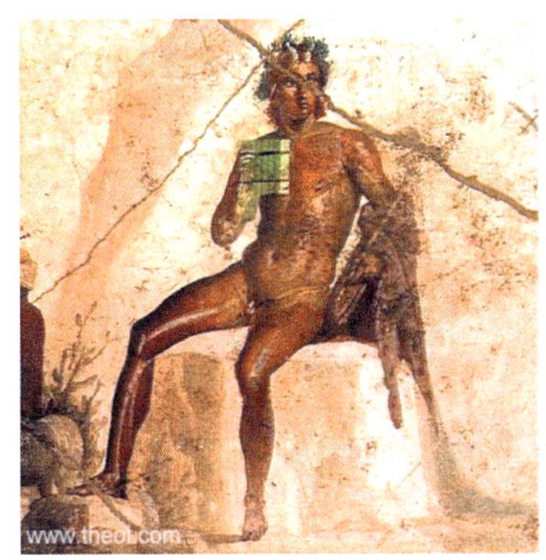

Pan as horned youth (with leopard skin of Dionysos, Pompeii, 1st A.D.

communities. The nymphs were depicted as human-like young women, the pans and satyrs as humanoids with horns, tail, beard, snub nose, ears, feet and legs like a goat. They were worshipped in forest groves and rock caves. The distinction between a demon and a god was that a god (θεός) emphasized his personality, and a demon his activity.

The earliest known version of the Narcissus story was told by Conon (63 B.C. – 14 A.D.), in a mythography of Greece titled *Narrations,* of which a 9th-century summary was preserved in the library of the patriarch of Constantinople. The story tells of a young man who was rejected as lover by Narcissus and called on the gods for revenge. The gods caused Narcissus to fall in love with his own reflection in the waters of a spring and he eventually killed himself. The flower that bears his name sprang up where his blood was spilled: "In Thespeia of Boeotia a child was born, Narcissus, very handsome and dismissive of Eros (god of love), and of lovers. While the others gave up, Ameinias kept insisting. Narcissus did not yield, but sent him a sword instead. He killed himself at Narcissus' doorway, after beseeching Eros to avenge him. Narcissus saw his own image reflected in a spring and became his first and only love… The locals believe that the narcissus flower first sprang up on that ground where Narcissus died."

The most widely known, and poetic, version of the Narcissus legend is found in Ovid's *Metamorphoses* (8 A.D.) Like Conon, Ovid did not cast Narcissus as a rustic spirit (δαίμον), but as a beautiful young hunter from Thespiae in Boeotia. He rejected the nymph Echo (actually his sister) and therefore was condemned by Nemesis (goddess of fate) to fall in love with his own reflection: "Now when Echo saw Narcissus, she burned with fire [and] came out of the woods to put her arms around his neck, but he ran away. As Narcissus scorned her, so he had scorned other nymphs and young men. One of them lifted his hands to sky and said: 'So may he himself love, and so may he fail to command what he loves!' The goddess Nemesis heard this just request. There was an unclouded fountain, and here Narcissus lay down to quench his thirst, when a different thirst was created. While he drank he was seized by the vision of his reflected form. He loved a bodiless dream. He thought a body what was only a shadow. He was astonished by himself, and hung there motionless. Flat on the ground, he contemplated his eyes, hair, cheeks, the beauty of his face. Unknowingly he desired himself, he inflamed and burned to embrace the neck he could see, he plunged his arms into the water. "Has anyone ever loved more cruelly than I? I am he. I sense it and I am not deceived by my own image. I am burning with love for myself. I move and bear the flames. What shall I do? Surely not court and be courted? Why court then? What I want I have. Oh, I wish I could leave my own body! Strange prayer for a lover, I desire what I love to be distant from me. Nor is dying painful to me, laying down my sadness in death. I wish that him I love might live on, but now we shall die united, two in one spirit… Narcissus pined away and died. And as when he was received into the house of shadows, he still gazed into the Stygian waters. His sisters, the Naiads, lamented, and Echo returned their laments. And when they prepared the funeral pyre, there was no body. Instead of his body, there appeared a flower with white petals surrounding a yellow heart."

In a third version by Greek traveler and geographer, Pausanias, (active 143–176 A.D.), *Description of Greece*, it says that it was likely that Narcissus, to console himself for the death of his beloved twin sister, his exact counterpart, sat gazing into the spring to recall her features, and died from grief: "There is another story about Narcissus, less popular indeed than the other, but not without some support. It is said that Narcissus had a twin sister; they were exactly alike in appearance, their hair was the same, they wore similar clothes, and went hunting together. The story goes on that Narcissus fell in love with his sister, and when the girl died, would go to the spring, knowing that it was his reflection that he saw, but in spite of this knowledge finding some relief for his love in imagining that he saw, not his own reflection, but the likeness of his sister."

Ovid's etiological legend of Narcissus' transformation into the flower contrasts with analogous stories involving Pan. While Narcissus eschews sexual partners, male or female, Pan tyrannizes Pitys, Echo, and Syrinx and numerous other nymphs with his libidinous lust. To escape his grasp, these nature beings are changed into a tree, the sounds of the forest, and the reeds from which Pan fashions his pipe to create the music expressing his never satisfied sexual frustration. The stories of Pan and Narcissus are intertwined by the shared character of Echo. The nymph who has been changed into sound by Pan, falls in love with Narcissus. But while Pan seeks physical gratification, Narcissus turns his longing inside and when he dies pining for the disembodied vision of his inner self, he metamorphoses into the chaste flower. According to Ovid, Narcissus's mother was told by the blind seer Tiresias that he would have a long life, provided he never recognized himself. This seems to suggest that self-knowledge was considered fraught, if not fatal. Tiresias warns against looking at oneself too deeply, lest he will die. The story may have derived from an ancient Greek belief (held in many primitive societies) that it is unlucky or even fatal to see one's own reflection (or have one's picture taken or likeness painted). The ancient Greek aphorism "know thyself" (γνῶθι σεαυτόν) was inscribed at the oracle of Delphi and at the temple of Apollo. Socrates exhorted his students that the "The unexamined life is not worth living." Sophocles' tragedy of *Oedipus Rex*, first performed around 429 B.C. at the theater of Dionysos in Athens, showed the heavy price paid by the hero for self-knowledge. In that story, too, the seer Tiresias warns against looking at oneself too deeply, lest one will face fateful truths about oneself. The legendary Tiresias was a clairvoyant, blind prophet of Apollo in Thebes, a complex liminal figure, both male and female, and at home among the gods, humankind, and the dead in Hades. He was blinded by the gods for revealing their secrets, and turned into a woman for seven years for disobedience. Tiresias' pronouncements were cryptic, but always revealed to be true in the end.

According to the Greek historian Plutarch (*De defectu oraculorum*, "The Obsolescence of Oracles"), during the reign of emperor Tiberius (A.D. 14-37), when news of Christianity spread through the Roman world, rumors of Pan's death came to one Thamus, a sailor on his way to Italy by way of the Greek island of Paxi: "The father of Aemilianus the orator, said that once upon a time in making a voyage to Italy he embarked on a ship carrying freight and many passengers. It was already evening when, near the Echinades Islands, the wind dropped, and the ship drifted near Paxi. Almost everybody was awake, and a good many had not finished their after-dinner wine. Suddenly from the island of Paxi was heard the voice of someone loudly calling Thamus, an Egyptian pilot. Twice he was called, but the third time he answered; and the caller, raising his voice, said, 'When you come opposite to Palodes, announce that Great Pan is dead.' On hearing this, all were astounded and reasoned among themselves whether it to carry out the order or to refuse. Thamus made up his mind that if there should be a breeze, he would sail past and keep quiet, but with no wind and a smooth sea about the place he would announce what he had heard. So, when he came opposite Palodes, and there was neither wind nor wave, Thamus from the stern, looking toward the land, said the words as he had heard them: 'Great Pan is dead.' Even before he had finished there was a great cry of lamentation, not of one person, but of many, mingled with exclamations of amazement. As many persons were on the vessel, the story was soon spread abroad in Rome, and Thamus was sent for by Tiberius Caesar. Tiberius became so convinced of the truth of the story that he caused an inquiry and investigation to be made about Pan; and the scholars, who were numerous at his court, conjectured that he was the son born of Hermes and Penelope." Many early Christians believed that the story heralded the coming of their savior. Christian historian Eusebius of Caesarea (260-340 A.D.) claimed that the death of Pan, imaged as the death of "all" (εν και παν), resulted from the exorcism by Christ of all pagan gods and demons (δαίμονες). What before had been sacred, was now construed as dimensions of evil.

Pan's elevation to cosmic stature (in the Orphic hymns) marks the highest stage of his development, but it also ushered in a new attitude which can be described as literary and speculative rather than as belief in the living god. The ancient goat-god had arisen from direct religious experience of the Arcadians on the Peloponnese peninsula in southern Greece more than a millennium B.C. Confronted with the active power that sustained their lives, peasant herders intuited a mysterious and frightening divinity, half goat, half man. Their Pan was real, they knew him and continually felt his numinous presence. Some three centuries before Christ, Orphic hymnodists joined the external characteristics of the goat-god to the abstract idea of indwelling, universal divinity (εν και παν). This absorption of the tangible rural deity into philosophical thought is no longer rooted in mythic intuition; rather it emerges from the logical argument of equating Pan-theism with pantheism because they match etymologically. Consequently, the Orphic Pan was more of a conceptual image than an active living being. Eventually his activities were completely allegorized. The Roman author Cornutus (flourished ca. 60 A.D.), in *Theologiae Graecae compendium* (Compendium of Greek Theology), for example, interpreted the lower goatish extremities of Pan as a representation of the earth, the upper human part as reason, and as the sway of heaven over earth.

What we see here is the "quiet revolution" described by C. S. Lewis in his *Allegory of Love* (1958): "We moderns are apt to take it for granted that the poet has at his command, besides the actual world and the world of his own religions, a third world of myth and fancy." At the beginning of any literature, however, only the first two are available to the poet. The third developed in paganism when the old gods ceased to be taken as gods and became figures of allegory. While the Norse deities were suppressed as devils and largely lost to poetry, in the classical world the gods were saved "as in a temporary tomb, for the day when they could awake again in the beauty of acknowledged myth and provide Europe with its 'third world' of romantic imagining."

In the mythological complex of Pan we can trace this process of progressive allegorization at all levels. The archaic god of shepherds died as a center of worship. But in art and literature, he left behind a numerous progeny of male and female pans, who were now often identified with satyrs, fauns, silvans, nymphs, and even human figures like Narcissus. Legends arose reinterpreting Pan's primordial relations with the spirits of nature in bucolic love stories casting him in the role of sentimental shepherd pining for the nymphs of the forest (Echo) and river (Syrinx), or the moon goddess Selene. In the retinue of Dionysos, Pan was frequently depicted as a small, rough and lecherous satyr. To this context belongs a story pitting Pan against Eros, the smooth-skinned and prissy child of Aphrodite. In Hesiod's Θεογονία (Theogony, 730-700 B.C.), Eros was described as the primeval power — cosmic Desire — by which order and cohesion were created from chaos. In Hellenistic literary tradition, Eros came to represent civilized, domesticated sexuality (Cupid), and in that role he inevitably defeated Pan, who now stood for coarse animal instincts he yearned to overcome. Famous examples of the allegorical use of the Pan myth are found in Ovid's *Metamorphoses*, Virgil's pastoral poems, Apuleius' *Golden Ass*, and in Plutarch's story of the death of Pan.

In 313 A.D., Roman emperor Constantine promulgated the Edict of Milan, legalizing Christianity on a par with other religions practiced in the empire. While this was an important development in the history of Christianity, it was not a total replacement of traditional Roman mythology with the Christian. In 476 A.D., Romulus, the last of the Roman emperors in the West, was overthrown by the Goths under Odoacer, who became the first Barbarian to rule in Rome. The order that the Roman Empire had brought to western Europe for a thousand years was no more, and with the end of the empire the stories of the classical gods became the source of polite art and literature rather than of living belief. On the other hand, the belief traditions surrounding Pan, the satyrs and nymphs underwent a profound transformation that can be traced in European folk belief well into the nineteenth century. In pre-industrial Norway, for example, people believed that the so-called "invisible folk" (*usynlige*) were fallen children of God inhabiting nature and pining for salvation. The pagan *daimones* expressing a deep symbiosis of humankind with nature, were assimilated into Christian belief in disobedient angels fallen from Grace. As the monotheistic deity replaced the classical pantheon, the goat-footed deity of shepherds, hunters, forests and mountains became a demon of nature in the Christian sense, and the figure of Pan associated with fertility and sexuality was assimilated to that of Satan. In *On the City of God Against the Pagans* (De civitate Dei contra paganos), Saint Augustine of Hippos (354-430 A.D.) called Pan's followers fallen angels in male (*incubi*) or female (*succubi*) form appearing in dreams to seduce men and women, thereby effectively demonizing human sexuality: "There is, too, a very general rumor, which many have verified by their own experience, or which trustworthy persons who have heard the experience of

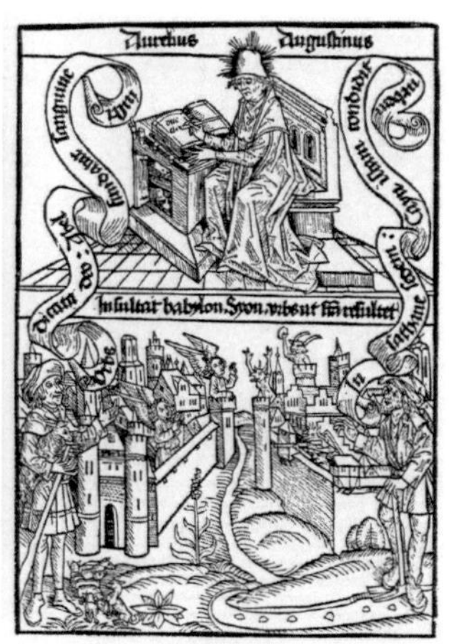

City of God, Woodcut
Johann Ammerbach, 1489

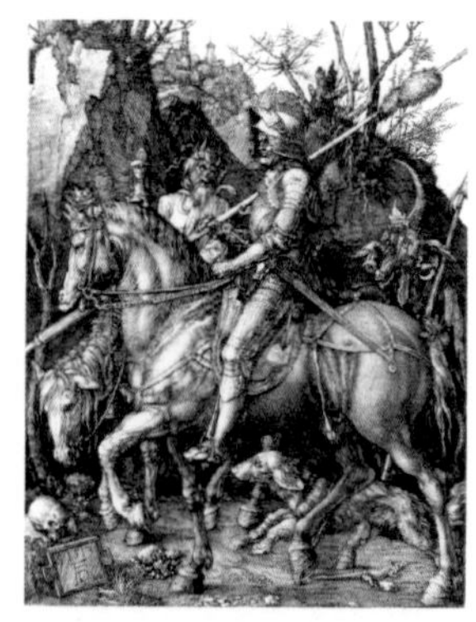

Knight, Death and Devil
Albrecht Dürer, 1513

others corroborate, that sylvans and fauns, who are commonly called incubi, had often made wicked assaults upon women [and men]." The image of Pan greatly influenced that of Satan in Christian art and literature. The goat-legged, pipe-playing god became the image of the devil.

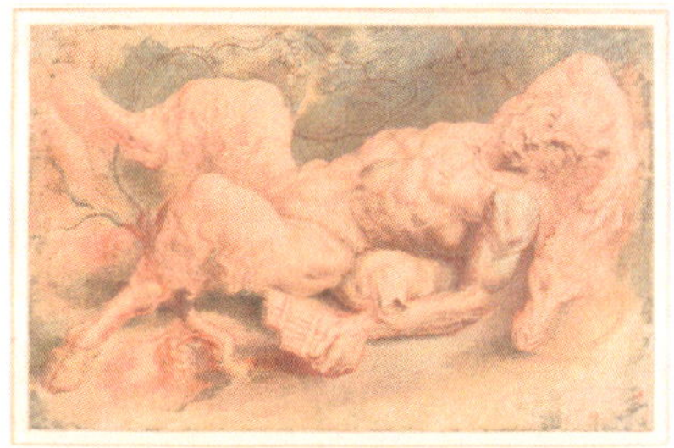

Peter Paul Rubens, *Red-Chalk drawing*, 1608

Not until the Renaissance did European artists recapture the figures of Pan and his retinue, including Narcissus, as the expression, if not of religious belief, but of the classical *joie de vivre* (joy of life) acceptable even to religious authorities. For instance, Peter Paul Rubens, a Catholic painter in Counter-Reformation Holland, went to Rome between 1600-1608, where he studied Renaissance masters such as Michelangelo, Titian, and Mantegna, as well as contemporaries such as Caravaggio.

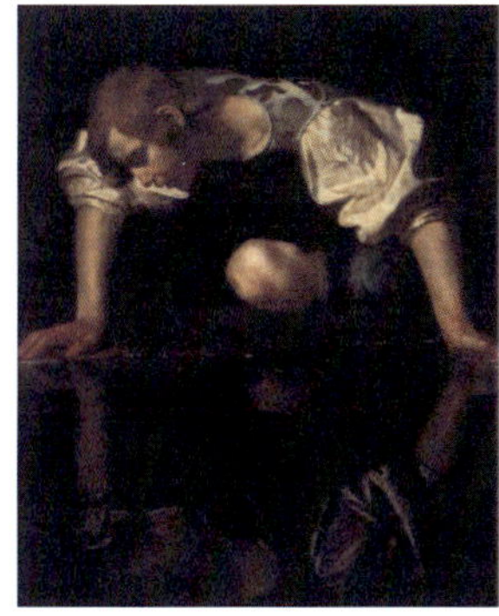

Caravaggio, *Narcissus*, 1599

In Michelangelo's studio he made a drawing of a Pan-sculpture commissioned by a patrician art collector, who later became Pope Urban VIII. The use of red chalk gives a realistic tone to the flesh of the supine bestial god sprawling among grapevines and resting his head on the body of a goat, giving it a sense of menacing life and movement ready to awaken from wine-induced torpor. Also Narcissus reappears in Renaissance iconography, as in Carravaggio's famous painting.

In the elegiac *À la forêt de Gastine* (To the Woods of Gastine) by Pierre de Ronsard (1524-1585), the French poet laments the failure of the woodsmen to realize that the trees are really divinities and the forest the home of fauns and satyrs. By contrast, English poet John Milton (1608-1674), in the ode "On the Morning of Christ's Nativity" (1629), incongruously suggests that while "leprous Sin will melt from earthly mould" as the "Moloch of yore"and idols of the pagan gods and oracles burn, "mighty Pan" is reborn as the Christ child (or at least the "simple" shepherds think so):

The shepherds on the lawn,
Or ere the point of dawn,
    Sate simply chatting in a rustic row;
Full little thought they than
That the mighty Pan
    Was kindly come to live with them below:
Perhaps their loves, or else their sheep,
Was all that did their silly thoughts so busy
keep.

Renaissance writers mostly employed the figures of Pan and Narcissus as decorative icons, or as emblems representing Nature. Roccocco poets and painters made use of the sentimental shepherd in their love idylls, as, for example, in Nikolas Poussin's *Écho et Narcisse*

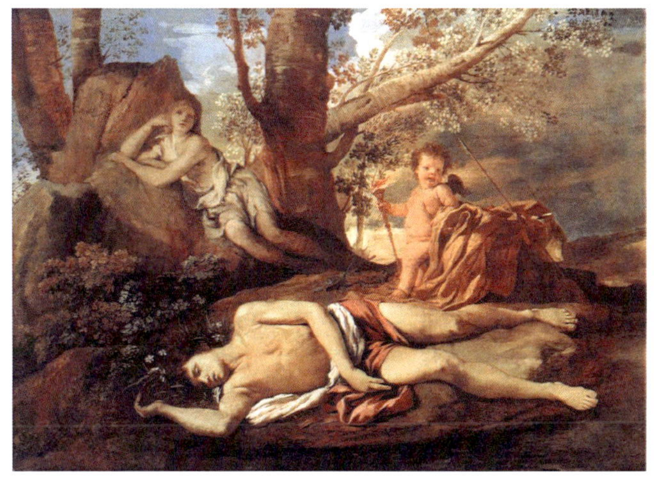

Nikolas Poussin, *Écho, Eros, and Narcissus*, 1628

(Echo and Narcissus), which shows the dead youth in the presence of the god of love (Eros) and the nymph, his sister Echo, whose passion he spurned.

 In contrast, the nineteenth century witnessed a comprehensive restatement of Pan and Narcissus as major mythological figures vested with modern thought and a new awareness of the psychological implications of the larger mythic complex.

In Goethe's *Faust* (1772-1831), for example, we encounter allegorical fauns, but the poet also creates striking new figures in which ancient mythological concepts are fused with new ideas. The figure of the Earth Spirit (*Erdgeist*) contains elements both of Arcadian Pan as numinous, active deity and of Orphic Pan representing the indwelling divine principle:

"Das All der Welt
Wird vorgestellt
Im grossen Pan…
In Lebensfluten, in Tatensturm
wall' ich auf und ab,
webe hin und her!
Geburt und Grab
ein ewiges Meer,
ein wechselnd Weben,
ein glühend Leben:
so schaff' ich am sausenden Webstuhl der Zeit
und wirke der Gottheit lebendiges Kleid."

(The All of the word/Is represented in the great Pan…/ In the flood of life, in the storm of deeds/ I flow up and down/ Blow to and fro!/ Birth and grave/ An eternal sea/ Ever-changing pattern/ Of radiant life:/ At the whirring loom of Time I weave/ The living garment divine).

Romantic writers from Rousseau to Emerson and Thoreau shared with Goethe the idea that nature is spiritual; they saw their role as prophet-poets to make sensitive and observant audiences aware that the world-soul could be experienced as presence in nature. Pastoral Pan became the symbol of nature in the poetry of Byron and Shelley. Wordsworth and Keats invoked the Orphic motif that Pan is "all" nature. Emerson, in *Nature* (1836) identified Orphic Pan with recurring cycles in nature and with the poet himself: "Standing on the bare ground, — my head bathed by the blithe air, and uplifted into infinite spaces, — all mean egotism vanishes. I become a transparent eye-ball; I am nothing; I see all; the currents of the Universal Being circulate through me; I am part or particle of God."

For Victorian poets the relationship to nature was rather more problematic. The Orphic totality held no reality for them. They chose instead the paradox of Pan being part goat and part man as an image to express a keenly felt conflict between hedonistic sensuality and conventional morality. In Robert Browning's *Pan and Luna* (1880), for example, the basic discrepancy lies between crude sexuality embodied in the goat-god and the poet's pathetic longing for a higher self represented by the chaste moon goddess:

"The purity we loved is gained for us.
So did girl-Moon, by just her attribute

Of unmatched modesty betrayed, lie trapped,
Bruised to the breast of Pan, half god half brute,
Raked by his bristly boar-sward while he lapped
--Never say, kissed her! that were to pollute
Love's language--which moreover proves unapt
To tell how she recoiled--as who finds thorns
Where she sought flowers--when, feeling, she touched—horns!"

Browning's poem reveals a prudish attitude toward sexuality commensurate with community standards during the Victorian period. After Queen Victoria (ruled 1837-1901) lost her beloved German husband, Prince Albert in 1840, she became a national icon identified with standards of sexual morality which today are generally considered prudish, suggesting fear and contempt of human sexuality and excessive female modesty. Women were to be undefiled, in marriage or without, while men were allowed access to prostitution in keeping with their presumably natural sexual needs. Thus prostitution, assumed only to be female, was tolerated, and legal throughout Europe. Prostitution was a major problem throughout the Victorian period, especially in growing cities and port towns.

Three remarkable art works by the English Victorians restore Narcissus' symbiotic relationship to nature lost in the poetic allegorization of the figure in Ovid's *Metamorphoses*. In Sir Edward Burn-

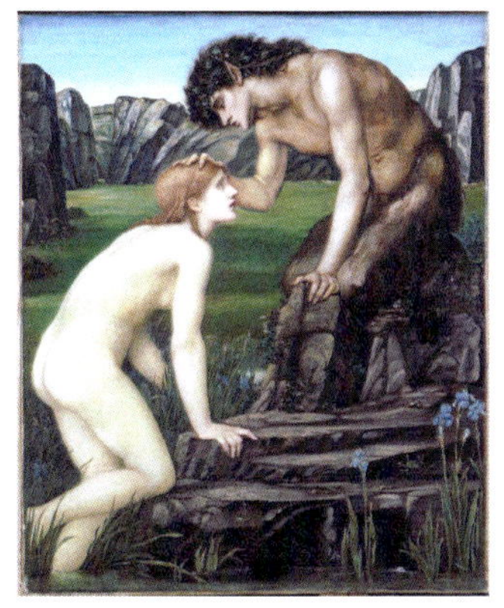

E. Burne-Jones, *Pan and Psyche*, 1874

Jones' *Pan and Psyche* (1874), Narcissus appears in the shape of Pan, beautiful in face and upper torso, with goatish legs and ears. He leans over the rock-lined spring from which an idealized, virginal female is emerging, which the artist calls Psyche. The spring is surrounded by beautiful blue Narcissus flowers. The painting expresses yearning rather than menacing instinct. The female leans forward toward the goat-man, who greets her gently, touching the top of her head. His body has earth tones, hers is pure white. An allegorical reading of this portrayal reflects a longing to transcend accepted social standards concerning sexuality. We notice that the female raised from the mirrored surface of the water is not the reflection of Narcissus himself, but Psyche, who in Greek mythology represents the human soul, mind, or spirit. In Jungian thought, the myth of Psyche was interpreted as the story of development of the feminine in the human self (see below). Thus Burn-Jones' rendering of the Narcissus legend can be read as an allegory of mature selfhood uniting male and female through mutual recognition in sexuality, in keeping with Plato's myth (Symposium) of humans being like two separated halves of an apple yearning to be reunited into one.

Another remarkable Victorian version of the Narcissus legend occurs in *Reflected Faun* (1894) by Laurence Housman, openly homosexual artist and feminist writer who reached his widest

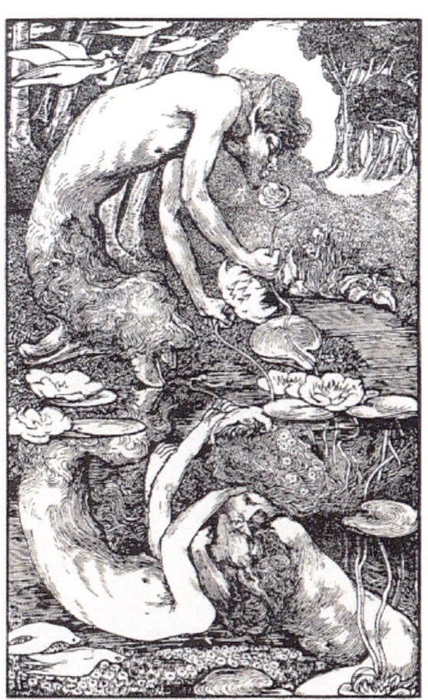

Laurence Housman, *Reflected Faun*, 1894

public with a series of plays about the Victorian era. Houseman brings together Ovid's Narcissus story as the lover who loves the image of himself with the larger story of the faun, satyr, or pan in which animal and human traits are combined to express a simultaneous self-identification with nature, as animal, and longing for transcendence, as human. The faun crouching by the pool raises a pond lily growing on the surface of the water to his lips. As he is about to kiss the flower, he sees his own reflection and that of the flower metamorphosed into a woman, or perhaps an androgynous being. Is it a nature being, a nymph, or Psyche rising from the depths of the unconscious as in the previous painting, or an imagined lover of the artist? Is the picture an allegorical appeal for acceptance of a wider understanding of human sexuality than allowed by the prevailing sexual mores during the Victorian era? The water lily the faun holds to his lips (*nymphaea nouchali*) has a beautiful white or blue flower and is native to the Indian subcontinent, an appropriate source of mythological imagery for a member of the British Empire. According to Buddhist lore, this flower was one of the hundred-and-eight auspicious signs found on Prince Siddhartha's footprint.

Thomas Sturge Moore, *The Pan Mountain* (1894). Moore was a prolific poet writing about morality, art and spirit, a wood engraver, and long-term friend and correspondent of W. B. Yeats, who thought of him as one of the finest poets in the English language. Moore's depiction of the flute-playing Pan as a menacing mountain figure reflects the topos in Romantic thought and literature representing the human heart as the deepest recess of the human self. 'Going into the mountain' meant to come into contact with mysterious powers, divine or demonic, and for the poet to be initiated into a journey to truth. In Novalis' novel fragment *Heinrich von Ofterdingen* (1798-1801), for example, the poet bathes in a subterranean stream of crystal water and there envisions the symbolic Blue Flower of self-realization and the infinite. By contrast, in Ludwig Tieck's *Der Runenberg* (Rune Mountain, 1797), the

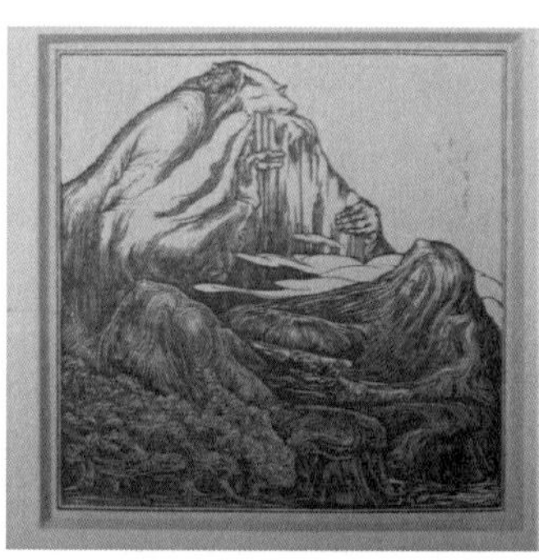

Thomas Sturge Moore
The Pan Mountain, 1894

mountain is identified with irrational forces lodged in sexuality. Tieck's use of the mountain symbol reflects themes in European folktales adumbrated in the medieval story of Tannhäuser, who is held captive in the mountain by the erotic spell of Venus, ancient goddess of love. In Adam Öehlenschlaeger's *Aladdin* (1807), the perilous journey into the mountain thematizes inner struggle. Hans Christian Andersen's *Rejsekammeraten* (The Traveling Companion, 1835) features a hero who in his dream frees the princess from the demon in the mountain. In Nordic folktales, to be 'taken into the mountain' (*å vare bergtatt*) meant to have lost one's mind under a sexual spell of the 'invisible' (*usynlige*), usually a nature demon in the illusory shape of a beautiful woman. In Henrik Ibsen's *Peer Gynt* (1865), Peer falls victim to the 'Green One' who lures him into the mountain, where he nearly loses his life. In Jonas Lie's *Jorden drar* (Pull of the Earth, 1892), an ordinary husband and father is slowly destroyed by a sexual power represented by an animal-like preternatural woman.

In the symbolism of Pan's Neo-Romantic revival at the end of the nineteenth century, the mountain becomes the metaphor for the unconscious. To the degree that the unconscious is dominated by the demonic Pan, its urges become potentially destructive to the individual and to society. T. S. Moore captures that sense of menace in his image of the mountain in the shape of Pan playing his entrancing tune on his pipes, a meaning captured by Knut Hamsun in his Symbolist novel *Pan* (1894, see below).

In French Symbolism, Pan and his retinue became the expression of the seesaw between body and spirit and intellect. Stephane Mallarmé's famous poem *L'Après-midi d'un faune* (The Afternoon of a Faun, 1887), allegorizes escape from physical sensuality into the rarified sensualism of the intellect and the imagination in the image of the faun as Narcissus' "illusion flowing from the blue and cold eyes of the chaste…like a weeping spring." Eduard Manet illustrated the scene, and Claude Debussy set it music to evoke "the faun abandoning himself to intoxicated sleep rich in dreams of possessing universal nature." In Germany, Arnold Böcklin, and other symbolist artists like Max Klinger, sought escape from intrusive industrialization in imagined mythic realities, including images recalling the world of Pan and Narcissus. In 1895, Klinger published a remarkable allegorical rendition of the Narcissus myth (completed ten years earlier) in the first volume of the newly established art journal *Pan*. Over the next five years, the journal became one of the most important voices in Europe of *Art Nouveau*, introducing contemporary major artists including Peter Behrens, Franz von Stuck, Klinger, Käthe Kollwitz, Auguste Rodin, Paul Signac and Félix Vallotton. Critical about the artistic policy of the German Empire under Wilhelm, the journal's financial backers were not interested in profit, but published to support young artists "without reference to commercial, moral, personal or polemical questions, appreciating only the purely aesthetic viewpoint." Not surprisingly, the venture proved not to be economically viable and had to stop publishing after five years, but is remembered today as "A Graphic Arts Time Capsule of

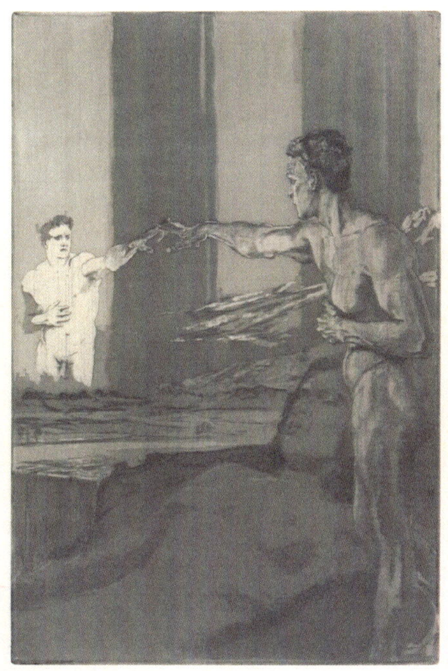

Max Klinger, *Narcissus as Philosopher*, 1885

Europe." The cover of the first volume shows the bestial face of Pan hovering menacingly over a distant horizon, while in front what seems a pond lily appears, its curved ovarian stigma in crimson red, the upright stamens spelling out the name of Pan, and the petals bearing the image of the bestial goat-god. In the middle ground, we see some tools of the gardener and the Pan pipes.

Klinger's aquatint etching shows a rough-hewn male human standing over a pool in which the body of a woman is seen floating, her eyes closed. The man points his outstretched fingers against a (glass?) surface in front of him, behind which the etherial mirror image of the man appears. Between them and partly behind the Narcissus figure, we see the broken stems and efflorescence of narcissus flowers. The title of Klinger's allegory ambiguously suggests that the fruit of Narcissus' self-reflection is philosophy (literally, "love of wisdom," or self-knowledge).

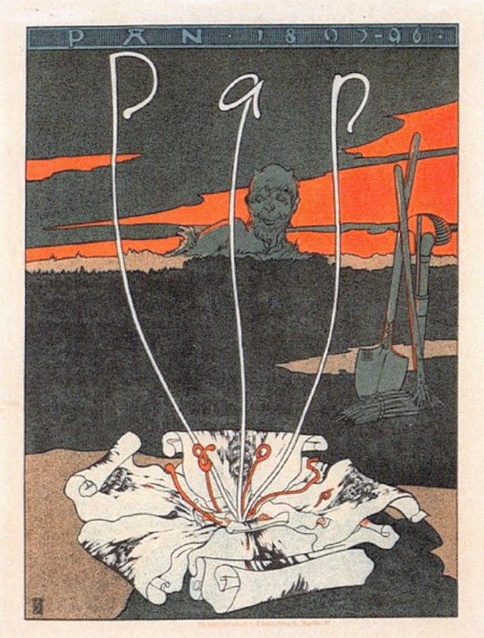

Pan, 1895-1900

Klinger was a close friend of Arnold Böcklin's, perhaps the most important northern European painter attached to the Symbolist movement, who in many allegorical paintings depicted aspects of emotional life through mythological imagery in the orbit of Pan and other figures from classical myth.

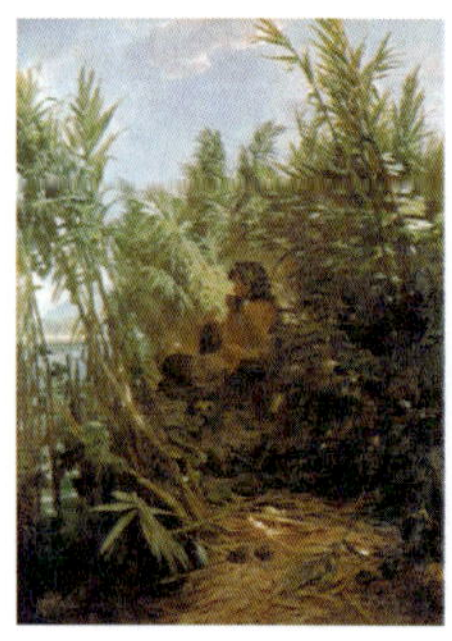

Melancholy, 1858

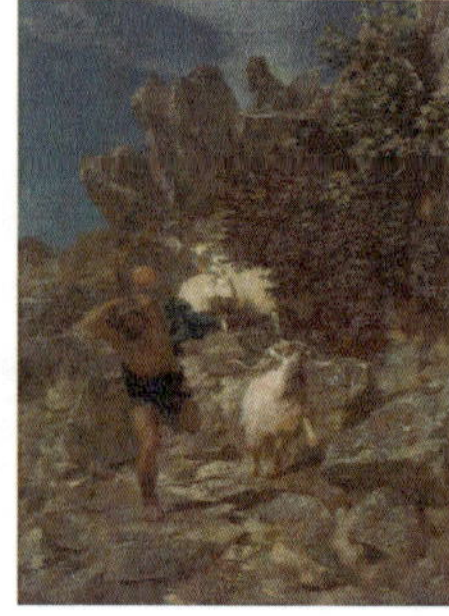

Panic, 1860

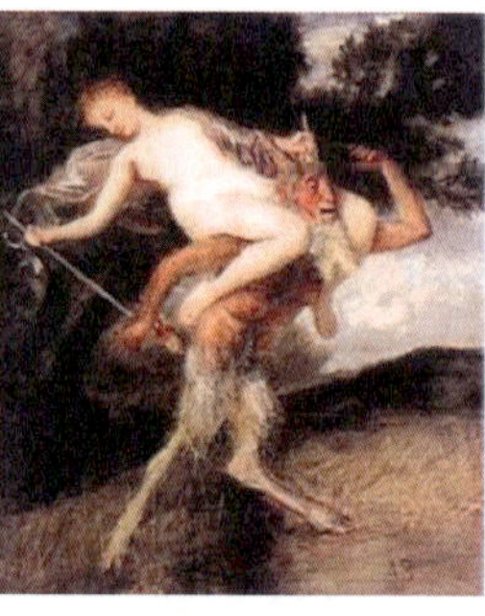

Sexual Torment, 1874

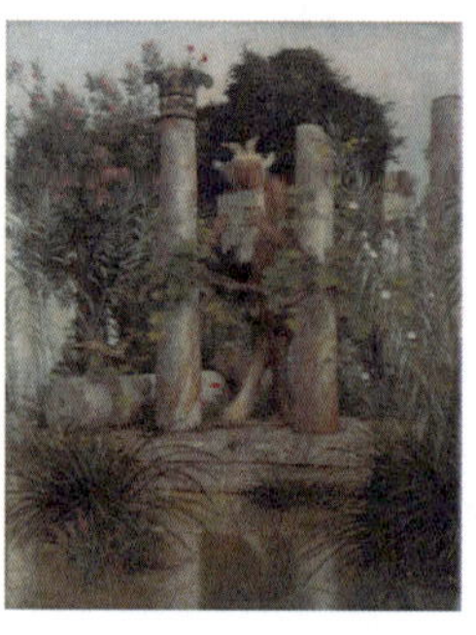

Contemplation, 1875

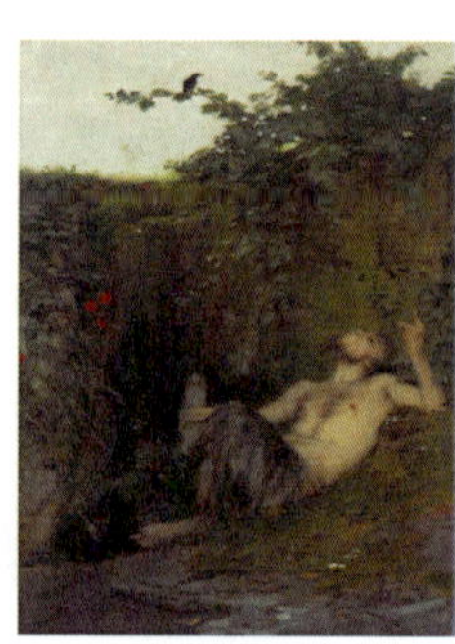

Teaching the Thrush to Sing, 1879

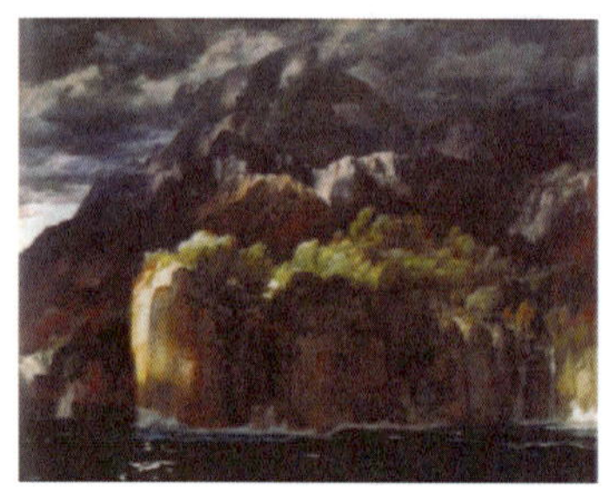

Chained on the Mountain, 1883

Böcklin's many interpretations of the goat-man show him alternately in his primitive Arcadian aspect, his mocking laughter sending animals and humans into headlong flight, or as Hellenistic satyr, as yet an animal in instinct but human in consciousness and therefore suffering. But unlike the Victorians, Böcklin was less concerned with moral conflict than with human isolation and shows the actual suffering caused by sexual conflict.

In Scandinavia, too, we can trace Pan's orbit in numerous poems from the 1880s-1890s. In Verner von Heidenstam's poems, the Dionysian satyr joins with man in an intoxicated dance against the death of the seasons. By contrast, Norwegian poet Nils Collett Vogt laments the death of great Pan as an irreparable, demonic, loss condemning modern man to sin, fear and death. The poetry of Danish Holger Drachmann and J. P. Jacobsen, pivots on the conflict between man's reason and deeper regions of self accessible only in moments of dreamlike experience. The satyr is inside the poet, and the lotus flower opening its blossoms for a moment reveals a "madman's eye."

The fullest mythopoeic expression of the many-faceted traditions of Pan, Dionysos, and Narcissus occurs in Knut Hamsun's novel *Pan* (1894). As a modernist exploration of the irrational self, it has been compared to the work of Joyce, Woolf, Kafka, and Proust. For Hamsun, myth captures *The Unconscious Life of the Soul* (1890): "The secret stirrings taking place, unnoticed, in the hidden parts of the soul; the incalculable chaos of perceptions, the delicate life of the imagination seen under the microscope, these wanderings of thought and feeling to unknown places, journeys of the brain and heart that leave no trace, strange reactions of nerves, the whisper of the blood, the prayer of our bones, the entire unconscious life of the soul…"

What follows are selected passages from the novel:

(Pan as sexual demon:) "…Soon there began to be no night; the sun barely dipped his face into the sea and then came up again, red, refreshed as if he had been down to drink. How strangely affected I was sometimes these nights; no man would believe it. Was Pan sitting in a tree watching to see how I would act? And was his belly open; and was he crouching so that he seemed to sit and drink from his own belly? But all this he did just to keep an eye cocked on me; and the whole tree shook with his silent laughter when he saw all my thoughts running away from me. In the first there was rustling everywhere; animals snuffled, birds called to each other, their cries filled the air. It was a year for Mayflies, their whirling mingled with that of the moths so that there was a sound of whispering back and forth all over the forest. How much there was to hear…"

(Pan and the chaste moon goddess Selene): "After an hour my senses begin throbbing in a definite rhythm, I am ringing with the great stillness, ringing with it. I look at the crescent moon stranding in the sky like a white shell and I feel love for it, I feel that I blush. 'It is the moon,' I say softly and passionately, 'It is the moon.' And my heart beats toward it with a slow throb…"

(Pan/Narcissus, and the nymph Syrinx): "And without saying more, she threw her arms violently around me, gazed into my eyes, breathing heavily. Her eyes were very black… 'It is late,' I said. 'The white flowers are closing again now, the sun is rising, the day is coming."

(Narcissus/dream of Iselin:)"…Something golden trembled within me. I stood before the mirror, and two love-lorn eyes looked out at me, I felt something moving within me as I gazed, trembling, trembling round my heart. Dear God, I had never seen myself with those eyes before, and in a rapture of love I kissed my own lips in the mirror…"

(Mountain symbol): "…Lull! Lull! Bells ringing? Some miles out to sea stands a mountain. I say two prayers, one for my dog and one for myself, and we enter the mountain. The gate slams behind us; I start at the sound and wake…" (But later the hunter drills in the mountain and blows it up, killing his lover).

(Orphic Pan:) "It was as if I lay face to face with the depths of the earth and as if my heart beat fervently against the naked depths and was at home there…This stillness murmuring against my ear is the blood of all nature seething, is God weaving through the world and me…A slight breeze springs up, a strange wind reaches me, a mysterious rush of the air. What is it? I look around and see nobody. The wind calls me and my soul bows willingly to the call and I feel myself lifted up, out of my context, pressed to an invisible breast, my eyes fill with tears, I tremble — God stands somewhere near and looks at me. Again it lasts a few minutes. I turn my head, the strange wind ebbs away and I see something like the back of a spirit wandering soundlessly into the forest…"

Another evocation of Orphic Pan is found in Hamsun's later novel *Siste Glæde* (Last Joy, 1912): "Something ripples softly through me, and I feel, as so many times before in the open fields, that someone has just left this place, that someone has just been here and has only stepped aside. At this moment I am alone with someone here, and shortly after that I see a back disappearing into the forest. It is God, I think to myself. I am standing there, I don't speak, I don't sing. I only see. I feel that my entire face is filled with what I see. It is God, I think. A vision, you say. No, just a little insight into things, I answer. Do I make god out of nature? What else are you doing? Do not the Muslims have their god, the Jews theirs, the Hindus theirs? Nobody knows God, little friend. Man knows only gods. And now and then I meet mine…"

Beyond poetry and painting, the myths of Dionysos, Pan, the satyrs, and Narcissus are explored in anthropological context in J.G. Frazer's *The Golden Bough* (1890), and in philosophical context in Friedrich Nietzsche's monumental *The Birth of Tragedy from the Spirit of Music* (1872/1886). Frazer assimilates the Arcadian and Hellenistic myths to those of the vegetation deities of the Near East whose tragic stories tell of their death with the coming of winter and their rebirth in spring. He attributes the origin of the story of Narcissus to myths common both in ancient India and in Greece that in looking at one's reflection in water the soul would be dragged under water by nature spirits, causing the person to perish.

Hamsun's contemporary, the philosopher Friedrich Nietzsche, made Dionysian Pan — Nietzsche calls him a Satyr — known in modern tradition. Nietzsche interprets the vision of Dionysos in everyday existence and cult as direct experiences of life's irrational, creative principle. According to Nietzsche, the Satyr was "the primordial image of man, the expression of his highest and strongest feelings; he was the traveler intoxicated by the divine presence, the sufferer reliving the agonies of the god, the prophet of nature's wisdom…the symbol of its universal sexual power…an amoral artist-god who in creation and destruction, for good or evil, realizes himself in tyrannical ecstasy." Civilized man seeks out Dionysos not only in religious cult but also in any mode of ecstatic states from nature, dance, and art experiences to sexual ecstasy and narcotic intoxication. In ecstasy the limitations of civilization are exploded, and the individual is cleansed and renewed. But in order to survive the state of ecstasy, the individual must be protected and led back to the norms of rational consciousness. Nietzsche designates this necessary rational principle Apollonian. Dionysos' gift is ecstasy, but Apollo creates the socially authorized norms of religious cult, art, and theater, designed to protect the individual against self-destruction.

The Neo-Romantic imaginings of the Symbolists came to an abrupt end by the eve of World War I. In 1899, Paul A. Näcke, a German criminologist, narrowly defined narcissism to describe someone who treated his own body as a sexual object, and connected this definition with criminal homosexuality. About the same time, British physician Havelock Ellis characterized narcissism as a mental disorder linked to an inflated self-image and addiction to fantasy. Both of these interpretations ignore the wider cultural meanings surrounding the mythological context of Pan, satyr, and Narcissus developed throughout Europe throughout the nineteenth century. Much of human experience beyond the sexual drive is lost from view. Forgotten is that Narcissus' looking deeply into the reflection of the unconscious, generates the beautiful flower variously interpreted by symbolists as the placement of the self between nature and cosmos, the feminine side of the masculine self, or personal truth in artistic or intellectual creation.

In *Introduction to the Concept of Narcissism* (1914), Sigmund Freud posits that narcissism is a necessary intermediate stage between auto-erotism and object-love. Freud distinguishes two phases of narcissism, one natural and healthy experienced in early childhood, the other pathological in the narcissist adult. In the process of ego- and superego-formation, the wishful libidinal dreams of 'His Majesty the Baby' run up against the social code imposed by parental authority. The gradual maturation of the child engenders a dynamic sense of guilt that is abated only as the child learns to transfer self-love to a love object outside itself. If libidinal development suffers some disturbance, the person becomes a narcissist in the secondary sense, a "person who treats his own body in the same way in which the body of a sexual object is ordinarily treated—who looks at it, that is to say, strokes it and fondles it til he obtains complete satisfaction through these activities. Developed to this degree, narcissism has the significance of a perversion that has absorbed the whole of the subject's sexual life, and it will consequently exhibit the characteristics which we expect to meet with in the study of all perversions…."

Freud holds further that affectionate parents who ignore the cultural constraints "their own narcissism has been forced to respect" interfere with the healthy libidinal development of the child. "Parental love, which is so moving and at bottom so childish, is nothing but the parents' narcissism born again, which, transformed into object-love [overweening love of the child], unmistakably reveals its former nature…" By 1930, Freud distilled the inherent conflict between parental love and their cultural responsibility to embed the social code in the child, into his analysis of what he calls the widespread "discontent" (*Unbehagen*) in modern culture. In essence, he argued, second stage narcissism has become a pervasive feature arising from social constraint in the modern world.

As noted by Freudian therapists and theorists (Baumann, Benzini, Charmico, Dell'Amico, Ellenberger, Fromm, Horney, Kernberg, Kohut, Lacan, Lasch, Lowen, Marcuse, Racalcati, Stiegler, Suttora, and many others), during the second half of the century since Freud's analysis, a major shift has taken place in Western culture, which can be summed up as the replacement of parental authority (representing the superego) by the authority of the marketplace representing the ego ideal embodied in popular culture, advertisement, and social media (Dell'Amico, 2022). New forms of both personal and general cultural suffering emerged primarily focussed from the paradigm centered on guilt to one focused on lack of self-esteem and shame. The pathology of narcissistic personality disorder morphed into the pathology of the narcissist consumer society (Kernberg, 1984).

The left-leaning student protests of the 1960s against all forms of authority interfering with individual self-development (family, society, government), the hippie and drug culture of the 1970s, the radical feminist movement questioning patriarchal power structures (Millet 1970, Firestone 1970), and the civil and gender rights movements, led to a fundamental cultural shift, where the individual self replaced the patriarchal model based on discipline, duty and sacrifice (Lacan 1968). Individual rights rose to the forefront over collective duty. Individual aspirations overtook family or community interests (Baumann 2000, Recalcati 2019).

On the level of the family, the child emerged as omnipotent subject whose self-individuation dominated by drives irreconcilable with the social group as in classical Freudian analysis was to be fostered, and its desires had to be protected from normative interventions by parents and institutions. In public education, respect for the singularity of everyone's desires, for nature, and for different cultures replaced assimilation of traditional canons on which Western civilization had been based for more than two millennia.

However, these developments inadvertently produced a progressive unmooring of the individual psyche (Charmet, 2019). Raised in the perspective of individual fulfillment, the child and adolescent clash with collective cultural models promoted by the flux of industrial *Ersatz* (substitute) products (Freud, 1938) offered by the mass media and the internet, with thousands of individuals emotionally synchronized as they watch the same violent images on their screens (Arendt, 1995, Virilio, 2012). Bereft of respect for parents and deprived of sublimations (superego cultural imagoes), the young desperately invent motives that lead to self-sabotage and suicidal tendencies. As Goethe said: "If you don't have 2,000 years at your finger tips, you're living hand to mouth" in the flat world of the moment, without the steadying models of the past, and without secure prospects for the future. At the same time, social conservatives push back against the weakening of moral and normative values constituting the superego, leading to the modern-day mixture of pretended respect for others and a striking rise in violence in human and social relations (Richard 2011). The pseudo-liberation of sexual practices is subtly obstructed by the requirement of the transparency of good intentions based on ideals of respect for others, while at the same time providing an apology for individual freedom ("my body, my freedom"), and not so subtly contravened by suppressive laws aimed at abortion, contraceptives, and gender fluidity. The current rash of mass shootings in America most likely is rooted in the cynical contradictions of contemporary social morality. Modern "liberation" has turned on itself (Stiegler, 2012). Latter-day narcissists stare at the pools of their screens, hoping to cure their neurosis of anxiety, depression, and isolation through virtual approval (Twenge, 2014, 2017, Akkoz, 2020).

In "On Narcissism: An Introduction," Freud (1914) had defined the ego ideal as the imago toward which the child turns to find self-love in interaction with authority figures. The inevitable conflict between ego and superego generated an abiding sense of "guilt" never fully relieved until the child matured to project its need for love on an outside object. A hundred years after Freud, by contrast, the conflict between ego and ego ideal is less associated with guilt than with the pervasive emotion of "shame" associated with a feeling of personal inadequacy (Suttora & Benzi, 2020). While guilt arose from the child's internal judgement of failing to conform to the expectations of parents, shame is generated by an external valuation of personal inadequacy to meet social standards promoted by the marketplace, popular entertainment, and media (McWilliams, 2011). A fear of being "unmasked" (for example by "ghosting") as socially inadequate contributes to the development of eating disorders, antisocial behavior or suicide attempts (Lancini & Cirillo, 2021). Among aspiring professionals, the so-called "impostor phenomenon" (Clance & Imes, 1978) appears increasingly widespread (Palmer, 2021). So-called *hikikomori*, a syndrome of shame first diagnosed in the 1980s and widely reported primarily among adolescent males, reveals a growing sense of lacking virility causing escape into the virtual world of violent computer games, sports heroes and pop stars (Tamaki, 2013). The constant threat of inadequacy in the face of social expectations fosters hyper-sensitivity in relationships and social withdrawal (Charmet, 2019). The need to conform to an internalized moral code, traditionally the product of norms set by parents, is replaced by the need for approval and external recognition of individual value and identity (Kohut, 1971-1982), and leads to narcissistic trends in the general culture (Lasch, 1979, Lowen 1983.) Since the 1950s, therapists were increasingly confronted with patients complaining of a chronic perception of emptiness, a meaningless life, and strong personal insecurity (McWilliams, 1999), a development that has been described as a "paradigm shift" (Kuhn 1962) from the "guilty man" to the "tragic man" model in the psychology of the self (Kohut, 1971, 1976, 1978, 1982, Kernberg 1975, 1976, 1984, Zoja 2016, Burgo 2016, Keohane, 2016, Richards 2018, Vater, 2018, Campbell & Crest, 2020). Especially in the United States, theorists have posited a broad cultural pathology they identify with Freud's definition of narcissism.

At the same time, while the cultural shifts described here are generally acknowledged by Freudian theorists and therapists, there have also been many who upheld cultural narcissism as a potentially positive phenomenon (Kohut 1971, 1977, 1978, 1982, Kernberg 1975, Lasch 1979, Burgo 2013, Arble 2014, Ngiam 2020). Some even speak of "healthy narcissism." By contrast, psychiatrists Henri F. Ellenberger (1979) and Anthony Stevens (1983) describe narcissism as a form of "creative illness" arising after long periods of intense intellectual work. Tobi Zausner, New York writer, artist and psychodynamic therapist invokes chaos theory to point out that many of the world's greatest masterpieces were inspired by an artist's poor health. Botticelli, Dürer, Michelangelo, Rembrandt, Titian, Goya, Monet, Matisse, Munch, Ryder, da Vinci, Kahlo, O'Keeffe, Matisse, and Dorothea Lange are among the many artists whose disorders ("chaos") enhanced their creativity and transformed their lives. Narcissism is here seen as a threshold experience that functions as a transition to a new stage of life and the production of new art.

In his monumental *The Discovery of the Unconscious: The History and Evolution of Dynamic Psychiatry* (1970), Ellenberger diagnoses the social malaise felt by Pre-Raphaelites in England, Symbolists in France, and *Jugendstil* adherents in Germany (he ignores the Scandinavians) as signs of sexual narcissism as narrowly defined by Freud a generation later. However, writers, artists and thinkers like Mallarmé, Debussy, Browning, Housman, Moore, Burn-Jones, Nietzsche, Böcklin, Klinger, Hamsun, Heidenstam, Vogt, Jacobsen, and Drachmann raise up the myth of Narcissus beyond the Freudian reading to encompass traditional associations with Pan, Dionysos, the Satyr, and other nature beings. The neo-romantics saw in Narcissus the possibility of life freed from the Freudian discomfort of civilization, and this perspective was continued by thinkers and artists in the 20th century. Marxist social philosopher Herbert Marcuse (1955), for example, saw Narcissus as the archetype of the revolt against the practice of self-alienating work and obligation to drive renunciation. To him, Narcissus becomes the image of desire emancipated from the ideological cage of society. Mythographer Joseph Campbell (1956) compared the legend of Narcissus looking into the pool to the story of "Buddha sitting contemplative under the tree, but it is not the ultimate goal; it is a requisite step, but not the end. The aim is not to *see*, but to realize that one *is* that essence; then one is free to wander as that essence in the world."

Salvador Dalí explores the linkage of the myth of Narcissus with self-reflection in artistic creation. Inspired by Böcklin's *Island of the Dead* (1880), the surrealist painter imagined Narcissus as bending over a pool, his head showing a fissure reproduced in the allegorical egg rising from the surface of the pool with a hand mirroring the shape of his body holding up an egg, from which the flower of his introspection arises. Dalí had read Freud's *The Interpretation of Dreams* as an art student in Madrid in the early 1920s. This was, he wrote, "one of the capital discoveries of my life, and I was seized with a real voice of self-interpretation, not only of my dreams but of everything that happened to me." His passion for self-interpretation took not just visual but also written form. In 1933 Dalí penned a "psycho-analytical essay" discussing self-interpretation through art in keeping with André Breton's *The Surrealist Manifesto* (1924), which defined surrealism as "Thought expressed in the absence of any control exerted by reason, and outside all moral and aesthetic considerations." In 1938, during a meeting with Freud in London to discuss the psychoanalytical theory of Narcissism, Dali sketched Freud in the shape of the same egg, suggesting the affinity of Freud's theory of Narcissus with the creative, interpretive process. The linkage of self-reflection with nature, the flower and the egg, is prominent in recent works by contemporary artists concerned about climate change and the human role in the natural environment. As climate philosopher Roy Scranton (2015) puts it: "We need to learn to see not just with Western eyes but with Islamic eyes

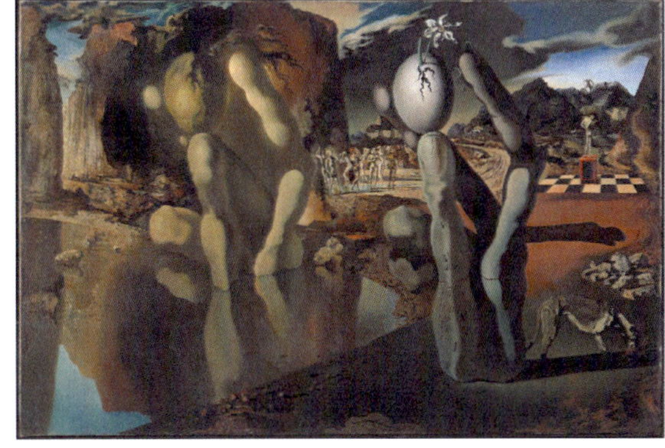

Salvador Dalí, Metamorphosis of Narcissus, 1937

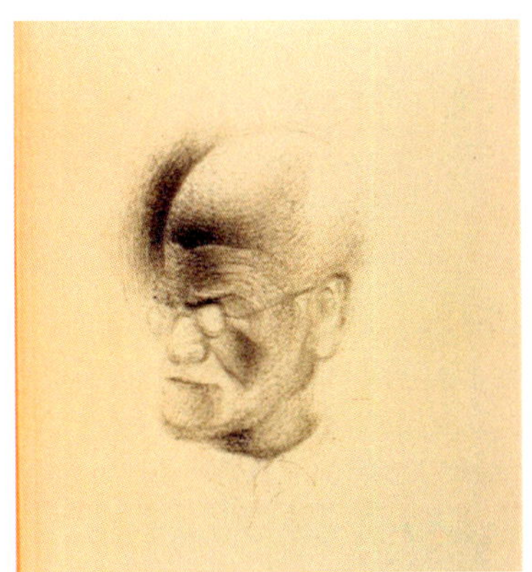

Dalí, Freud as Egg, 1938

and Inuit eyes, not just with human eyes but with golden-cheeked warbler eyes, coho salmon eyes, and polar bear eyes, and not even just with eyes at all but with the wild, barely articulate being of clouds and seas and rocks and trees and stars." Since 2011, Norwegian artist Caroline Hjorth and her Finnish colleague Rita Ikonen have undertaken an ongoing collaborative project that started out as a play on Nordic folklore, but has morphed into a continual search for modern humanity's belonging to nature by portraying mostly old people from all over the world as solitary figures in a landscape dressed in flowers and other natural elements shaped in egg form. The figures become sculptures enacting nature both in content and context.

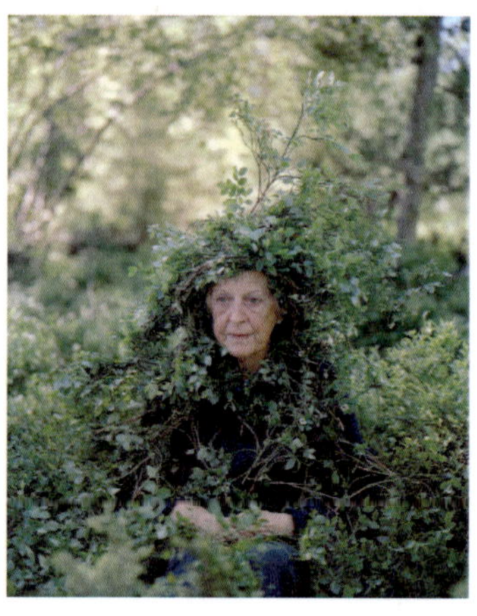

C. Hjorth & R. Ikonen
Eyes as Big as Plates, 2017

C. G. Jung would argue that the images of the flower and the egg arise from the collective unconscious in which archetypes of the human Self reside and are precipitated in mythology, fairy tales, art, philosophy, and symbolic dreams prompting the individual across cultures toward individuation. Like any educated man at the time, Jung was conversant with the mythological and philosophical traditions of ancient Greece and Rome, and he was able to read and write both languages. He also was an avid student of Friedrich Creuzer's massive *Symbolik und Mythologie der alten Völker, besonders der Griechen* (Symbolism and Mythology of the Ancients, particularly the Greeks, 1910-1912), a four-volume archeological and philological study that described and interpreted the ancient myths and legends in detail. In his clinical work with the patient, Jung early on was struck how their dreams reproduced mythological themes and motifs, leading him to understand such projections as expressions of universal contents arising from the collective unconscious. Unlike the concept of the personal unconscious popularized by both Freud and Jung, the collective unconscious is not the repository of thoughts, memories or ideas of which an individual had been conscious during his life but forgotten or repressed. Rather the collective unconscious contains inheritable universal elements that are common to all humans by virtue of shared general psychological development, brain and nervous system development, evolutionary biology, and the history of civilizations. The collective unconscious "consists of pre-existent forms, the archetypes, which can only become conscious secondarily and which give definite form to certain psychic contents" (Jung, 1959). While Freud was wholly concerned with personal psychology based on instinct, Jung emphasizes the universal physiology common to all humans. He does not deny "instincts"as motivating urges, but posits the collective unconscious as a universal causal frame in the human species, while instincts are present in all species. It is pertinent to note that one of Freud's motives in writing his *Introduction* was, as he said, to show that the concept of narcissism offers an alternative to Jung's "non-sexual libido," i.e. to the notion of the collective unconscious. Freud (1927) held that the ancient gods had slowly "withdrawn," abandoning humans to their "helplessness" (*Hilflosigkeit*), while Jung insisted that the "gods" continued to inform human consciousness collectively, and the purpose of therapy was to help individuals access those framing forms.

By contrast, as early as 1908, Freud referred to the "modern" neurosis (*Nervosität*) "rapidly spreading in our present-day society," which he connected with the constant acceleration of human activity in the major cities of the twentieth century and the repression of the sexual drives as the source of the anxiety of "cultural discontent." Later he linked the modern neurosis with pathological failure of libidinal development. In 1914, Freud wrote: "We have discovered, especially clearly in people whose libidinal development has suffered some disturbance, such as perverts and homosexuals, that in their later choice of love-objects they have taken as a model not their mother but their own selves. They are plainly seeking themselves as a love-object, and are exhibiting a type of object-choice which must be termed 'narcissistic'. In this observation we have the strongest of the reasons which have led us to adopt the hypothesis of narcissism." Jung, too, considered homosexuality the result of psychological immaturity, but emphasized that it should not be considered a crime or of any concern to legal authorities, nor somehow reduce the value of the person as a member of society (Hopcke, 1988).

In contrast to Freud, narcissism is not a major framing concept in Jung's theory of the Self, but he does address the myth of Dionysos, Satyr and Narcissus in a number of contexts. In *Psychological Types* (1971) Jung writes: "The Dionysian impulse means the liberation of the dynamism of animal and divine nature. Hence in the Dionysian rout man appears as satyr, god above and goat below…an explosion of the isolated ego through the world…alienated Nature celebrating her reconciliation with Man."

Freud's concept of narcissism reflects a biological, sexual, and medical emphasis. Jung takes a different view and is critical of the prominence of narcissism in behavioristic analysis. Jung sees the negative Freudian critique of the introverted (narcissistic) personality as a reflection of a generalized cultural preference in the West for extraversion. In *Mysterium Conjunctionis* (The Mystery of Conjunction, 1956), Jung writes: "In general, meditation and contemplation have a bad reputation in the West. They are regarded as a particularly reprehensible form of idleness or as pathological narcissism. No one has time for self-knowledge or believes that it could serve any sensible purpose. Also, one knows in advance that it is not worth the trouble to know oneself, for any fool can know what he is. We believe exclusively in doing and do not ask about the doer, who is judged only by achievements that have collective value. The general public seems to have taken cognizance of the existence of the unconscious psyche more than the so-called experts, but still nobody has drawn any conclusions from the fact that Western man confronts himself as a stranger and that self-knowledge is one of the most difficult and exacting of the arts."

In *Psychology and Religion: West and East* (1958), Jung elaborates: "Even a superficial acquaintance with Eastern thought is sufficient to show that a fundamental difference divides East and West. The East bases itself upon the psychic reality, that is upon the psyche as the main and unique condition of existence. It seems as if this Eastern recognition were a psychological or temperamental fact rather than a result of philosophical reasoning. It is a typically introverted point of view, contrasted with the equally typical extraverted point of view of the West. Introversion and extraversion are known to be temperamental or even constitutional attitudes which are never intentionally adopted in normal circumstances. In exceptional cases they may be produced at will, but only under very special conditions. Introversion is, if one may so express it, the "style" of the East, an habitual and collective attitude, just as extraversion is the "style" of the West. Introversion is felt here as something abnormal, morbid, or otherwise objectionable. Freud identifies it as an autoerotic, "narcissistic" attitude of mind."

In *The Spirit in Man, Art, and Literature*, (1922-1941) Jung writes: "[Freudian analysis] brings the work of art into the sphere of general human psychology, where many other things besides art have their origin. To explain art in these terms is just as great a platitude as the statement that "every artist is a narcissist." Every man who pursues his own goal *is* a "narcissist" — though one wonders how permissible it is to give such wide currency to a term specifically coined for the pathology neurosis… The reductive method of Freud is a purely medical one, and the treatment is directed at a pathological or otherwise unsuitable formation which has taken the place of normal functioning. It must therefore be broken down, and the way cleared for healthy adaptation."

In *Civilization in Transition* (1918-1959), however, Jung adopted Freud's use of the term narcissism to describe "morbid sexuality:" "Finally the word 'love' must be stretched still further to cover all sexual perversions. There is incestuous love, and a masturbatory self-love that goes by the name of narcissism. The word 'love' includes every kind of morbid sexual abomination as well as every kind of greed that has ever degraded man to the level of a beast or a machine."

On the whole, however, Jung considered Freud's use of the term "narcissism" reductive and limiting, and therefore less than helpful in many therapeutic contexts.

Most psychotherapists today find compatibility between narcissism as narrowly defined by Freud and personal affirmation. The *Diagnostic and Statistical Manual of Mental Disorders* of the American Psychological Association (2013) reports how many highly successful individuals express personality traits that could be considered narcissistic in the narrow Freudian sense. Only when these traits impair the individual's adaptation to its environment, can one speak of dysfunctional narcissistic personality disorder. Some therapists speak of "highly functioning narcissists" whose narcissism serves professional and personal achievement (Westen, 1990).

Jung's perspective on Narcissus locates the myth in the context of humankind's placement between its natural, physical being and its longing for spiritual transcendence expressed in mythology, art, music, philosophy and religion. Narcissus belongs into the orbit of the god, half goat and half human, half nature and half spirit. The surface of the water into which Narcissus stares represents the liminal boundary between the conscious and the pre-conscious before such terms were available to myth-makers. Narcissus looks within. Jung makes the case that in the modern, materialistic and science-based world narrowing abstractions replace mythic vision, but the pre-conscious, collective forms of the vision continue to shape our dreams and art. The inner vision of Narcissus produces the chaste flower.

Secondary Sources Consulted:
Anders, G. 1956. The Antiquated Being of Man.
Akkoz, M., & O. Erbaş. 2020. The Relationship Between Social Media Use and Narcissism.
Arble, E., & D. Barnett. 2014. An Analysis of Self: The Development and Assessment of Measuring Self-Object Needs.
Arendt, H. 1950. Introduction into Politics: The Promise of Politics.
Bauman, Z. 2003. Liquid Love: On the Fragility of Human Bonds.
Bauman, Z. 2000. Liquid Modernity.
Benasayag, M. & G. Schmit. 2003. The Age of Sad Passions. Mental Suffering and Social Crisis
Breton, A. 1924. The Surrealist Manifesto.
Burgo, J, 2013. Is There Such a Thing as Acceptable Narcissism?
Burgo, J. 2016. The Narcissist You Know: Defending Yourself Against Extreme Narcissists in an All-About-Me Age.
Campbell, Joseph 1945. The Hero With a Thousand Faces.
Campbell, W. K. & C. Crist. 2020. The New Science of Narcissism: Understanding One of the Greatest Psychological Challenges of Our Time—and What You Can Do About It.
Ciaramelli, F. 2000. The Destruction of Desire. Narcissism in the Age of Mass Consumption.
Clance, P.R., & S. A. Imes 1978. The Imposter Phenomenon in High Achieving Women: Dynamics and Therapeutic Intervention.

Colamedici, A. & M. Gancitano. 2018. The Performance Society.

Creuzer, F. 1910-1912. Symbolism and Mythology of the Ancients, especially the Greeks. 4 vols.

Dalí, S. 1933. Psycho-Analytical Essay.

Ellenberger, H.F. (1970). The Discovery of the Unconscious: The History and Evolution of Dynamic Psychiatry.

Firestone, S. 1970. The Dialectic of Sex: The Case for Feminist Revolution.

Franco, Angeli & J. Russell. 2021. Sublimation and Superego: Psychoanalysis Between Two Deaths

Frazer, James G. 1951. The Golden Bough: A Study in Magic and Religion.

Freud, S. 1899. Interpretation of Dreams.

Freud, S. 1905-6. Psychopathic Characters on the Stage.

Freud, S. 1908. 'Civilized' Sexual Morality and Modern Nervous Illness.

Freud, S. 1911. Formulations on the Two Principles of Mental Functioning.

Freud, S. 1914. On Narcissism: An Introduction.

Freud, S. 1921. Group Psychology and the Analysis of the Ego.

Freud, S. 1927. The Future of an Illusion.

Freud, S. 1929. Civilization and Its Discontents.

Freud, S. 1938. Findings, Ideas, Problems.

Fromm, E. 1956. The Art of Loving.

Fromm, E. 1964. The Heart of Man. Its Genius for Good and Evil.

Gabbard, G.O. & H. Crisp. 2018. Narcissism and Its Discontents.

Galimberti, U. 2010. The Disturbing Guest. Nihilism and Young People.

Gauchet, M. 2010. The Advent of Democracy: The Test of Totalitarianism.

Goldberg A., D.R. Rigney & B.J. West. 1990. Chaos and Fractals in Human Physiology.

Green, A. 1993. The Work of the Negative.

Gribinski, M. 2011. Fragments of the New World.

Hopcke, R. 1988. Jung and Homosexuality: A Clearer Vision.

Feltrinelli, H. 1975. The Age of Sensation: A Psychoanalysis Exploration.

Jung, C.G. 1912 Psychology of the Unconscious.

Jung, C.G. 1918-1959. Civilization in Transition.

Jung, C.G. 1921 Psychological Types.

Jung, C.G. 1922-1941. The Spirit in Man, Art, and Literature.

Jung, C.G. 1952 Symbols of Transformation.

Jung, C.G. 1956 Mysterium Coniunctionis.

Jung, C.G. 1958. Psychology and Religion: West and East.

Jung C.G. 1962. Dreams, Memories, Thoughts.

Jung, C.G. 1964. Man and His Symbols.

Jung, C.G. 2009 The Red Book: Liber Novus (posthumous)

Jung, C.G. 2020 Black Books (posthumous).

Keohane, K. 2016. The Social Pathologies of Contemporary Civilization.

Kernberg, O.F. 1992. Aggression in Personality Disorder and Perversions.

Kernberg, O.F. 1975. Borderline Conditions and Pathological Narcissism.

Kernberg, O.F. 1976. Object Relations Theory and Clinical Psychoanalysis.

Kernberg, O.F. 1984. Severe Personality Disorders.

Kernberg, O.F. 2018. Treatment of Severe Personality Disorder.

Khun, T.S. 1962. The Structure of Scientific Revolutions.

Kohut, H. 1971. The Analysis of the Self.

Kohut, H. 1977. The Restoration of the Self.

Kohut, H. 1978. The Search of the Self.

Kohut, H., & Wolf, E, S. 1978. The Disorders of the Self and their Treatment: An Outline.

Kohut, H. 1979. The Two Analyses of Mr Z.
Kohut, H. 1982. Introspection, Empathy and the Semicircle of Mental Health.
Lacan, J. 1968. Note on the Father and Universalism.
Lasch, C. 1979. The Culture of Narcissism.
Lewis, C.S. 1958. Allegory of Love.
Lingiardi, V. 2021. Variations On Narcissism.
Lingiardi, V. & N. McWilliams (eds.) 2017. Psychodynamic Diagnostic Manual (PDM).
Lowen, A. 1983. Narcissism. Denial of the True Self.
Lütz, M. 2020. Dr. Kernberg: What Is Psychotherapy For?
Marcuse, H. 1955. Eros and Civilization: a Philosophical Inquiry into Freud.
Marcuse, H. 1964. One Dimensional Man: Studies in the Ideology of Advanced Industrial Society.
McWilliams, N. 1999. Psychoanalytic Case Formulation.
McWilliams, N. (2011). Psychoanalytic Diagnosis. Understanding Personality Structure in the Clinical Process.
Miller, A. 1979. Prisoners of Childhood.
Miller, J. D., M. D. Back, D.R. Lynam & A.G. Wright 2021. Narcissism Today: What We Know and What We Need to Learn.
Millet, K. 1970. Sexual Politics.
Ngiam, J. 2020. Narcissism: Heinz Kohut's Thoughts on Self-Love. Is Narcissism Really Bad?
Palmer, C. 2021. How to Overcome Impostor Phenomenon.
Pietropolli Charmet, G. 2019. The Unbearable Need for Admiration
Recalcati, M. 2019. The Telemachus Complex: Parents and Children after the Decline of the Father
Reich, W. 1930-36. The Sexual Revolution.
Richard, F. 2011. Malaise in Culture Today.
Richards, B. 2018. Exploring Malignancies: Narcissism and Paranoia Today.
Rosci, E. 2003. Hurting, Getting Hurt. Teens Attacking the World and Themselves.
Scranton, R. 2015. We're Doomed. Now What?
Sehmsdorf, H. 2022. The Mirrored Faun: Knut Hamsun's *Pan* and the Myth of the Unconscious.
Slater, P.E. 1970. The Pursuit of Loneliness: American Culture at the Breaking Point.
Stevens, Anthony 1983. Archetypes: A Natural History of the Self.
Stiegler, B. 2012. Uncontrollable Societies of Disaffected Individuals: Disbelief and Discredit.
Suttora, C. & I.M.A. Benzi, 2021. Narcissism in Developmental Age and Adolescence. In: Madeddu, F. (ed.), The Thousand Faces of Narcissus: Fragility and Arrogance Between Normality and Pathology.
Tamaki, S. 2013. Hikikomori: Adolescence Without End.
Twenge, J.M. 2014. Generation Me: Why Today's Young Americans Are More Confident, Assertive, Entitled and More Miserable Than Ever Before.
Twenge, J.M. 2017. Have Smartphones Destroyed a Generation?
Twenge, J.M. & W.K. Campbell 2009. The Narcissism Epidemic: Living in the Age of Entitlement.
Vater, A., S. Moritz & S. Roepke. 2018. Does a Narcissism Epidemic Exist in Modern Western Societies? Comparing Narcissism and Self-Esteem in East and West Germany.
Vegetti Finzi, S. 1990. History of Psychoanalysis.
Virilio, P. 2012. The Administration of Fear: Intervention Series.
Westen, D. 1990.The Relations Among Narcissism, Egocentrism, Self-Concept, and Self-Esteem: Experimental, Clinical, and Theoretical Considerations.
Zausner T. 1998. When Walls Became Doorways: Creativity, Chaos Theory, and Physical Illness.
Zoja, L. 2000. Hector's Gesture: Pre-History, History, Modernity and the Disappearance of the Father.